MYSTERY AND MAGIC

Step-by-Step Science Activity Projects
from the Smithsonian Institution

Gareth Stevens Publishing
MILWAUKEE

For a free color catalog describing Gareth Stevens' list of high-quality books, call 1-800-542-2595 (USA) or 1-800-461-9120 (Canada). Gareth Stevens' Fax: (414) 225-0377.

Library of Congress Cataloging-in-Publication Data

Hands-on science: mystery and magic / by Megan Stine . . . [et al.] ; illustrated
   by Simms Taback.
         p.   cm. -- (Hands-on science, step-by-step science activity projects from
      the Smithsonian Institution)
      Series originally published by the Smithsonian Institution as a series of science
activity calendars.
      Includes bibliographical references and index.
      Summary: Presents a variety of activities, experiments, and simple tricks that
explore principles of electricity, physics, biology, and more.
      ISBN 0-8368-0958-0
      1. Science--Experiments--Juvenile literature.   2. Scientific recreations--Juvenile
literature.   [1. Science--Experiments.   2. Scientific recreations.   3. Experiments.]
I. Stine, Megan.   II. Taback, Simms, ill.   III. Series: Hands-on science
(Milwaukee, Wis.).
Q164.H245   1993
507'.8--dc20   92-56893

Produced and published by
Gareth Stevens Publishing
1555 North RiverCenter Drive, Suite 201
Milwaukee, Wisconsin 53212, USA

This edition © 1993 by the Smithsonian Institution. First published by
the Smithsonian Institution and Galison Books, a division of GMG Publishing,
as a series of Science Activity Calendars.

Series editor: Patricia Lantier-Sampon
Book designer: Sabine Beaupré
Editorial assistants: Jamie Daniel and Diane Laska

Printed in the United States of America

2 3 4 5 6 7 8 9 9 99 98 97 96 95 94

CONTENTS

Weights and Measures Abbreviation Key

U.S. Units

in = inch	oz = ounce
ft = foot	qt = quart
tsp = teaspoon	gal = gallon
T = tablespoon	lb = pound
C = cup	°F = °Fahrenheit

Metric Units

cm = centimeter	kg = kilogram
m = meter	km = kilometer
ml = milliliter	°C = °Centigrade
l = liter	
g = gram	

INTRODUCTION

By the 21st century, our society will demand that all its citizens possess basic competencies in the fundamentals of science and technology. As science becomes the dominant subject of the workplace, it is important to equip children with an understanding and appreciation of science early in their lives.

Learning can, and does, occur in many places and many situations. Learning occurs in school, at home, and on the trip between home and school. This book provides suggestions for interactive science activities that can be done in a variety of settings, using inexpensive and readily available materials. The experiments, activities, crafts, and games included in this book allow you, whether teacher or parent, to learn science along with the children.

SOME SUGGESTIONS FOR TEACHERS

The activities in this book should be used as supplements to your normal classroom science curricula. Since they were originally developed for use in out-of-school situations, they may require some minor modifications to permit a larger number of children to participate. Nonetheless, you will find that these activities lend themselves to a fun-filled science lesson for all participants.

SOME SUGGESTIONS FOR PARENTS

One of the most important jobs you have as a parent is the education of your children. Every day is filled with opportunities for you to actively participate in your child's learning. Through the **Hands-On Science** projects, you can explore the natural world together and make connections between classroom lessons and real-life situations.

FOR BOTH TEACHERS AND PARENTS

The best things you can bring to each activity are your experience, your interest, and, most importantly, your enthusiasm. These materials were designed to be both educational and enjoyable. They offer opportunities for discovery, creative thinking, and fun.

HOW TO USE THIS BOOK

There are ten activities in this book. Since every classroom and family is different, not all activities will be equally suitable. Browse through the book and find the ones that seem to make sense for your class or family. There is no prescribed order to these activities, nor any necessity to do all of them.

At the beginning of each activity is a list of all the materials you will need to do the project. Try to assemble all of these items before you begin. The procedures have been laid out in an easy-to-follow, step-by-step guide. If you follow these directions, you should have no difficulty doing the activity. Once you have completed the basic activity, there are also suggested variations that you can try, now or later. At the end of each activity is an "Afterwords" section to provide additional information.

SUPER SLEUTH

SUPER SLEUTH

3 in x 5 in = 7.6 cm x 12.7 cm
8 1/2 in x 11 in = 21.6 cm x 27.9 cm

Snooping, sneaking, and sleuthing are a lot of fun, but harder than you think. It will take you 90 minutes to collect your suspects' fingerprints and solve the crime.

YOU WILL NEED

Lipstick or an inked stamp pad (Carter's Micropore or similar non-reinkable pads are easiest to clean off)

Package of 3" x 5" plain white file cards

Several sheets of 8½" x 11" paper

Pen

Paper towels, soap, and water for clean-up

There are more than 200 million fingerprint cards on file with the FBI. Do you think the police look at each one every time they want to identify a fingerprint found on a smoking gun? At that rate, the police would only solve about one crime every 10 years! In fact, there's a system that helps detectives locate fingerprints pretty quickly. Find out how fingerprints are sorted and classified by doing a little criminal-science work of your own.

FINGERPRINTING THE SUSPECTS

1 Make and label a bunch of blank fingerprint cards like the ones shown on this page. You'll need two blank cards for each person in your family — one for the right hand and one for the left hand.

2 For the next few steps in this activity, you'll want to have a sink, paper towels, and soap nearby. Starting with your right hand, ink your thumb on the stamp pad, or lightly cover your thumb with a thin coating of lipstick. Be sure to get the ink or lipstick on the *sides* of your thumb — not just on the flat part. To do this on the ink pad, you'll have to roll your thumb from one side to the other. You can help one another with the finger rolling.

3 Now practice making a thumbprint by rolling your thumb the same way on a piece of white paper. If you can clearly see the details of your thumbprint on the paper, you're ready to begin filling in your fingerprint card. If not, keep practicing until you can make good, clear fingerprints without smearing.

4 Now ink your thumb again and roll it on the square labeled "thumb" on the Right Hand card marked with your name. Continue making fingerprints on the cards until you have a complete set — right and left hands — for each person in your family.

HINTS FOR SUCCESS

■ You should ink only one finger at a time — otherwise you'll smear ink all over the cards by accident.

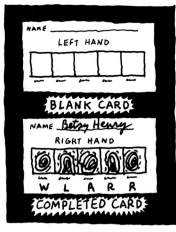

ARCH | WHORL | RIGHT LOOP | LEFT LOOP | UNKNOWN

- When you roll your thumb or finger from one edge to the other in the ink, press *lightly* so that you don't pick up too much ink.
- Press *firmly* when you roll your thumb or finger onto the labeled card. That way, you're less likely to move your finger and smear the print.
- If the "ridges" on your fingers don't show up well when you ink them, soak your fingers in hot water for a minute or two before trying to ink them again.

CLASSIFYING THE PRINTS

5 Look at your fingerprints and compare them with the print types shown in the chart. Decide whether each print is an Arch, a Whorl, a Right Loop, or a Left Loop. Sometimes a fingerprint will look like an Arch to one person and a Whorl to another, so discuss the classifications with everyone in your family and go with the majority vote. If you can't agree on a type for a particular fingerprint, mark it with a U for Unknown.

Mark the first letter of the print type under each fingerprint on your card. Use A for Arch, W for Whorl, and so on.

COMMITTING THE CRIME

6 Choose one person to be the detective and send that person out of the room. Decide what kind of crime you want to commit, and choose someone to be the criminal. You can make up a story to go along with the crime, but the important thing is that the criminal must leave his or her fingerprints on a piece of white paper. Draw a picture of a weapon, a drinking glass, an envelope, or whatever else might go along with your crime scenario, on a piece of white paper. If you can't think of a crime, you might draw a picture of a safe, like the one shown here.

7 One by one, ink the fingers of the criminal's right hand, and put his or her fingerprints on the drawing of the weapon, safe, or whatever. Be fair about it, or your detective will never solve the case! Put the criminal's fingerprints on the drawing in the right order — thumb, index finger, middle finger, ring finger, and then pinkie. Secretly

send the criminal to wash his or her hands. (Or better yet, have *everyone* go to the sink, just so the detective won't overhear anything and guess who the criminal is!)

8 Now call the detective back into the room and let him/her classify the prints on the drawing, writing the appropriate letter under each print. When all five prints have been classified, the detective should be able to look at the sequence of letters and match it to an *identical* sequence on the fingerprint cards you've all made.

VARIATION

Real fingerprints are invisible — until you dust them with a fine powder to make them show up. Find out how much harder real-life detective work is by collecting and classifying some real-life prints!

■ Scrape some pencil lead across an emery board, letting the fine black powder fall into a dish.

■ Use a soft watercolor brush and very carefully "dust" the powder onto a drinking glass you've touched. The powder will stick to the oil mark your fingers made.

■ Place a piece of clear tape on the dusted print, press lightly, and then lift the tape off. Save your lifted fingerprint by taping it on a clean card.

■ Play Super Sleuth the *hard* way. When you're out of the room, have a member of your family secretly leave a single "mystery" print on a clean glass. See how long it takes you to find its match on the fingerprint cards.

AFTERWORDS

Long before fingerprints were accepted as a means of identifying criminals, a Frenchman named Alphonse Bertillon developed an identification system of his own. Bertillon's method, adopted in 1882, was based on the idea that each person's physical measurements were unique. When a criminal was brought to the French police division where Bertillon worked, he would take a set of eleven measurements, including the length of the torso, hands, legs, feet, etc. These measurements remained on file and helped the police identify repeat offenders.

Although Bertillon's system was widely used for about 30 years, it was eventually abandoned because it

wasn't accurate in every case. Fingerprints then became the preferred method of identification. William Herschel is credited with developing a practical fingerprinting technique, which he used in Bengal, India, in the 1850s, even before the Bertillon system was adopted in Europe. But Sir Edward Richard Henry, who was Herschel's successor in India, came up with a way to *classify* the prints.

The classification system developed by Sir Henry is still in use in America today. It consists of a series of numbers and letters written like a fraction, with the symbols for the right hand appearing above the line and the symbols for the left hand appearing below. For instance, a typical fingerprint code would look like this:

$$\frac{5 \text{ Ar-r } 12}{17 \text{ T-2r}}$$

The first number in the classification is a code that tells whether or not there are whorl patterns in the set of prints. Other letters stand for various pattern types, and some parts of the classification even involve counting the ridges in a particular print! This is a slow, painstaking process, best done

with a magnifying glass.

When the police find a fingerprint at the scene of a crime, the first thing they do is classify the print. If there is a suspect handy, the police can fingerprint that person and carefully compare the prints to see if they match. But more often than not, the suspects are *not* handy. Then the police must turn to the fingerprints that are *already on file*. Even these filed fingerprints would be useless if they weren't classified. Sir Henry's classification system is so complete that police can quickly find a similar set of prints by simply looking through the code numbers. Then, and only then, the careful visual identification process begins.

Of course, fingerprints aren't the only unique physical characteristics that can be used to identify people. Newborn babies are always footprinted immediately after birth, to ensure that there will be no "mix-ups" in the nursery. The noseprints of dogs are equally unique, and so are certain boney projections on horses' legs. But our Super Sleuths are content with a system that's right at their fingertips.

MAGNETIC PERSONALITIES

MAGNETIC PERSONALITIES

Do you want to go north, south, east, or west? This one-hour activity can head you in the right direction — by teaching you how compasses work.

YOU WILL NEED

20 or 30 Little magnets (see **Note**)
5 or 6 Plastic soda straws, jumbo size
Thread
Paper clip
Cardboard box
Needle
Scissors
Tape (Duct tape works best.)
Steel sheet of some kind (baking sheet, cookie-tin lid) or iron frying pan
Small plastic container with lid (like a ½-pound margarine tub) or a clear plastic soda bottle
Felt-tip marker

Note: Radio Shack sells three kinds of little magnets: doughnut-shape ones, rectangular ones with holes in the center, and tiny ones with no holes. Get 10 of each if you can, but be sure to get several of the smallest.

Since their early discovery, the mysterious properties of magnets have served people in many ways. Magicians have used them to dazzle audiences with seemingly impossible stunts. Magnets are also necessary for navigating ships and planes: They are what make compasses work. Share in some of the mystery and make a compass of your own.

1 Put the doughnut magnets on a pencil. Reverse every other one so that all of them *repel* (push away from) each other. Hold the pencil upright, like a flag pole. Now hold the pencil horizontally and compare the spacing between the magnets. How do you explain the difference?

2 Amaze your friends! Carve away all but one layer of the cardboard in a small area on one size of a cardboard box *from the inside.* Tape a doughnut magnet there. Tape a few more doughnuts to it. Turn the box over so the magnets in the box are a secret that only you know about. Tie a paper clip to a piece of thread, and tape the free end of the thread to the table. Stick the clip to the box, right where the magnets are hidden, and carefully push the box away until the clip is suspended in thin air!

3 Magnets will either *attract* or *repel* each other, depending on which "poles" are brought together. Can you figure out whether it is two *like* poles or two *opposite* poles that attract? **Hint:** You'll need *three* magnets to solve this little problem.

4 Tape 3 or 4 magnets, one each, to the end of 3 or 4 straws. (Or just slip doughnut magnets over straws and wrap tape around the straw ends so the magnets won't fall off.) Use equal lengths of thread to suspend the straws in space from the end of a ruler. Make sure they

4.

are all positioned exactly in a line so that the magnets *repel* when they hang next to each other. If you suspend them above a steel sheet or iron pan, you can set other magnets underneath; these will also affect the swinging magnets. Experiment to see how long you can keep the magnets swinging. If you place them just right, you may discover *perpetual motion* — the magnets may swing forever!

5 Now make your own compass. Cut a 2" or 3" piece of straw and cut a point on one end. Cut a notch in the center of the piece as long as the thickness of 2 little round magnets.

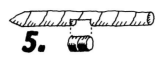

5.

6 Poke (or drill) a tiny hole in the center of the bottom of the plastic container and a little hole in the center of the lid, too. Thread the needle with about 18" of thread, and run it up through the hole in the bottom of the container. Tape over the end of the thread *and* the hole securely.

6.

YOU CAN USE YOUR COMPASS TO FIGURE OUT DIRECTIONS

GIVE DIRECTIONS FOR SOMEONE TO FOLLOW

SEE MAP BELOW ↓

7 Trap the thread between two of your little magnets, run the needle through the middle of the notch in your straw pointer, and out through the hole in the lid.

7.

8 Push the pointer down over the magnets, and push the whole thing down into the center of the container. Fill it with water, put the lid on, and tape the thread on the top. Don't pull

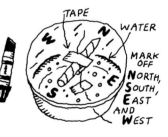

TAPE   WATER

MARK OFF **N**ORTH, **S**OUTH, **E**AST AND **W**EST

TREASURE HUNT
GO EAST INTO FRONT ROOM. TURN NORTH OUT DOOR. GO WEST TO TREE. GO EAST TO BUSH. TURN WEST TO GARAGE.

ST/86

the thread very taut! (It's a little more difficult, but you can follow the same procedures to build your compass in a plastic soda bottle.) **Note:** The compass *will* work without water in the container, but water keeps the pointer from swinging too much.

9 Now you've finished your compass! Because the pointer always points north, you can figure out the other directions and use a felt-tip marker to mark off north, south, east, and west on the compass lid. Then organize a treasure hunt! Give clues with directions like "Go north to tree. From there, go west to door." Let a friend borrow your compass to find the treasure.

AFTERWORDS

The Greek island of *Magnesia* gave magnets their name. The legend goes that in ancient times shepherds grazed their sheep on this island. Each shepherd carried a wooden walking stick, or *staff*, and covered the end with iron so it wouldn't wear out so quickly on the rocky ground. The shepherds then noticed that some of the tiny stones in the soil would cling to the iron tips but would not stick to the wood itself.

Later in history but still a long time ago, Norsemen (people from what is now Norway, Denmark, and Sweden) invented the earliest compasses. The Norsemen were excellent sailors who knew how to guide their ships by the stars — especially the Norse, or "North," Star. But if the stars were hidden by fog or clouds, this *stellar navigation* was impossible. Then the Norsemen noticed that a certain type of rock, if allowed to move freely, would always point north, toward the North Star. One of the earliest compasses was made from a piece of this *lodestone,* or "leading stone." The rock was set in a block of wood and then set afloat in a basin of water. As the earth's magnetic field pulled on the lodestone, the wood would turn to point north — the direction of the magnetic field.

Other *magnetic substances* act like the lodestone. These include *ferromagnetic* metals such as iron, nickel, and cobalt. *Ferro* means "iron," and as it turned out, lodestone is a highly concentrated form of magnetic iron ore. By combining some of the simpler ferromagnetic metals, modern man can create powerful magnetic materials.

If you pick up a magnet shaped like a candy bar, you will find that its magnetic effect is mainly found near the ends — the *poles* of the magnet. There are two types of magnetic poles, and one of the laws of magnetism states that two *like,* or similar, poles will repel each other and two *unlike* poles will attract.

Finding out which pole is which can be a little tricky. First you must know that the half of the Earth nearest the North Star is called the Northern Hemisphere. The Earth's axis "sticks out" in the Northern Hemisphere at the *geographic North Pole.* One pole of a free-moving magnet will always point toward a spot nearby this North Pole. This spot is called the *magnetic North Pole.* The end of the magnet that points toward this pole is called the *north-seeking pole.* But, because unlike poles attract, the north-seeking pole of the magnet must actually be the *magnetic South Pole.* Whew! The best way to avoid confusion is to remember that all magnets in the Northern Hemisphere are labelled "north."

Even scientists do not yet completely understand magnetism. They believe that magnetism is determined by the tiny particles, or atoms, that make up the magnetic substances; pairs of electrons orbiting around the nucleus of the atom may cause magnetism. This may be why, if you take your candy-bar magnet and break it in half, you end up with *two* magnets, each with two poles.

Magnetic substances that keep this magnetism going in one direction are called *permanent magnets.* The Earth itself is a huge permanent magnet; its *magnetic field* acts between its magnetic North and South Poles. A compass works because its magnetic needle is attracted by the Earth's magnetic field.

Permanent magnets are a part of your everyday life. They are at work in electric motors, stereo speakers, telephones, televisions, and even in some refrigerator doors!

> 2 in = 5.1 cm
> 3 in = 7.6 cm
> 18 in = 45.7 cm
> 1/2 lb = .226 kg

SCIENCE MAGIC

SCIENCE MAGIC

Hocus pocus! It's time to focus on magic! You can learn to do all the tricks for this magic act in about 45 minutes. But it might take you longer to perform the best all-time disappearing trick—the one that makes your stage fright disappear!

YOU WILL NEED

Tray for props
5 Pennies
Plate
Raisins
Club soda
Several drinking glasses
Water
Handkerchief

ADVICE TO AMATEUR MAGICIANS

Some of the tricks you are about to learn have been used for many years by famous magicians. And yet they are very simple to do! But the first time you try these tricks, they may not seem totally amazing to your friends. Why not? For two reasons: One is that you need to practice them many times, so that you can do them smoothly and confidently. And the other thing you need, in order to really come off like a polished magician, is patter. Patter is all the small talk magicians make while they are performing the trick—or waiting for it to work! So be sure to use lots of snappy patter while performing your tricks. (But don't tell anyone we told you—because that's a trick of the trade!)

GOOD VIBRATIONS: A MIND-READING COIN TRICK

Have 4 or 5 pennies ready, each with a different date. *Make sure you don't handle the pennies too much!* You might even want to put them in the refrigerator for a few minutes before the magic show. Put the pennies on a plate and ask someone from the audience to choose one, while your back is turned. Tell them to hold the penny tightly to let their "vibrations" flow into the penny. Then tell them to look at the date on the penny, so they'll know which one they chose. After about 20 seconds, have the person pass it to someone else in the audience and go through the patter again—asking the second person to let their "vibrations" flow into the penny and to concentrate on the date. Now have the second person put the penny back on the plate and then tell you to turn around. Quickly you will identify the correct penny!

How It's Done:

You will quickly pick up or touch each penny until you find the one that is warmer than the others. Copper is a good conductor of heat—and all those "vibrations" are really just body heat, transferred from the person to the penny!

THE LIVING RAISINS

This is a quick but dumb trick, so don't spend too much time on it. Just try to make your patter cute.

Tell your audience that you have trained six raisins to think of themselves as fish. They are now, believe it or not, The Living Raisins. And you can prove it by returning them to their natural habitat: water. They love the water, you say, but like all fish they must have oxygen to breathe. And since they don't have gills, they will have to come to the surface for air. Also, you might add that The Living Raisins are from California, and consequently they prefer mineral water or seltzer rather than plain water.

Pour a glass of fresh club soda and drop six ordinary raisins into it. Then simply watch the action! The raisins will rise to the surface and then sink again repeatedly. Announce grandly, "The Living Raisins, ladies and gentlemen!" And then move on to another trick!

QUICKIE TRICKY

Choose a volunteer from the audience and have the person come forward. Tell the volunteer that you're going to do a mind-reading trick. Then turn around so that your back is to the person and close your eyes. Tell the person to put one hand on his or her head, and then to concentrate on whichever hand it is. Use a lot of patter for this trick—because you need about 30 or 45 seconds for the trick to work. Keep saying, "Are you concentrating on the hand?" Finally, tell the volunteer to put his or her hand down. Then turn around and quickly ask to see both hands—palms up. Miraculously, you will announce which hand was on the person's head!

How It's Done:

The palm that is lighter in color will be the one that was on the person's head. Why? Because blood didn't circulate as much in the hand that was up in the air.

DRAGON BREATH

Tell the audience that you have Dragon Breath, which allows you to heat things up simply by blowing on them. In fact, you say, you can make water boil in a glass just by touching it with your finger—once your finger has been heated up with Dragon Breath, of course.

To perform the trick, have a small glass of water and a *wet* handkerchief ready. The glass of water should be about two-thirds full. Cover the glass with the handkerchief and push it down into the glass until the cloth touches the surface of the water. Then hold the glass as shown, with one hand flat over the mouth of the glass and the other hand tightly wrapped around the handkerchief and glass, near the rim. Turn the glass over quickly. A little water might

PICK A PENNY AND HOLD IT TIGHTLY AND...

LET THE VIBRATIONS FLOW INTO IT!

HAVE YOU EVER TRAINED A PET?

WELL... I HAVE TRAINED THESE RAISINS.

PUT-YOUR HAND ON YOUR HEAD AND CONCENTRATE ON YOUR HAND!

I HAVE MY BACK TO YOU AND I AM NOT LOOKING.

RAISINS

GOLDEN SUN

ST 88

HANKERCHIEF AROUND GLASS | **TURN GLASS UPSIDE-DOWN** | INDEX FINGER

come out, but most of it will stay in the glass.

Now take away one hand—the one that was flat over the opening. Hold the glass and handkerchief near the rim—still upside down—and breathe your Dragon Breath on the index finger of your free hand. Then push down on the top of the glass (it's really the bottom, but it's upside down). Say, "Boil, boil, boil and bubble." The water should start bubbling, but if it doesn't, breathe on your finger again and push harder. Hold tight. The glass must slip down a little but the handkerchief must not move for the "boiling" effect to happen.

MAGICIAN'S NO. 1, MOST IMPORTANT RULE IN THE WHOLE WORLD

Never repeat a trick!

AFTERWORDS

Here are the secrets to the other amazing tricks in your Science Magic Show. It's up to you whether or not you want to reveal to your audience just how these spectacular tricks work.

The Living Raisins

The club soda you used for this trick contains a lot of bubbles, which are really the gas *carbon dioxide.* Bubbles tend to collect on the surfaces of things. So when you dropped raisins into the glass, the bubbles collected on the raisins and lifted them to the top of the liquid. But at the top, the bubbles break and the carbon dioxide is released into the air, so the raisins sink back down again.

Why do the bubbles lift the raisins up? Because when they attach themselves to the raisin, they increase the raisin's volume without increasing its weight very much. Now that the raisin-plus-bubbles is bigger, it displaces more water. Things that displace enough water to equal their own weight will float. So the "bigger" raisin will float. When the

bubbles that were clinging to the raisin burst at the surface, the raisin becomes smaller. Now it doesn't displace enough water to equal its own weight, so it sinks. This trick can also be done with salted peanuts and any carbonated soft drink.

Dragon Breath

Oooh...there are so many mysteries about this trick! Why doesn't the water fall out of the glass when you turn it upside down? That's easy: It has to do with *surface tension.* Have you ever noticed that you can fill a glass of water *past* the rim and it won't overflow? Water molecules tend to want to stay together rather than separate. So when you carefully add more water to the glass, the surface bulges up but doesn't spill over because the molecules would rather stick together than spread out all over the place. That's surface tension. In the Dragon Breath trick, you've got surface tension— even with the glass upside down. The water fills in each tiny space between the handkerchief, and creates

hundreds of little areas with enough surface tension to keep the water in the glass.

But what makes the water seem to boil? Air pressure, coming from outside the glass, is pushing up on the handkerchief and the water. When you push down on the glass, you cause the water level to drop and you create a space where there isn't any water. So air flows in through the handkerchief to equalize the pressure inside the glass. As the air moves up through the water to reach the "empty" space at the top of the glass, it looks like the water is boiling. And *you* look like a magician!

EYE CATCHERS

EYE CATCHERS

Your eyes help you to know what is going on around you. But sometimes your eyes can play tricks on you. Investigate your eye, and its tricks. This activity will take about 40 minutes.

YOU WILL NEED

Ruler
2 Cereal boxes, paring knife
Scotch tape, aluminum foil, wax paper
Large safety pin or small nail
Magnifying glass, if you have one
7 Pennies
Penlight
2 Pencils, paper, cardboard, pushpin
Green, black, and orange paints, crayons, or felt-tip markers
Flashlight or table lamp

1 Is seeing believing? Take a good look at the top hat at right. How does its width compare with its height? Measure it and see. Surprised?

RULER

2 It's a topsy-turvy world! Things aren't always as they seem. Cut the flaps off one end of a cereal box and tape a sheet of wax paper over the opening. Make a hole about the size of a dime at the center of the other end of the box; tape a 1″ × 1″ piece of aluminum foil over the hole.

WAX PAPER FOIL WITH PIN HOLE

CEREAL FLAKES

Use a big pin or small nail to poke a hole through the foil covering the hole. Light a birthday candle. (Be careful to keep hair and clothing out of the way.) Put the pinhole near the flame on the wax-paper screen. Move the box back and forth to sharpen the image. Blow gently toward the flame. Which end of the flame is up? Your iris works the same way with light rays coming from a distance.

LOOK 2 TO 3 FT. AWAY

Now, hold a magnifying glass at arm's length and look at something 2 or 3 feet away. Which way is up? The lens of your eye does the same trick when you look at something nearby.

3 Do you have smart pupils? Your pupil looks like a little black circle in the center of each eye. It

PENLIGHT

controls the amount of light that enters. Stand in front of a friend who is looking straight ahead. Turn on your penlight and bring it slowly from behind your friend's head around to the front. What happens to the size of your friend's pupil as the light gets closer? As it moves away?

4 Light that enters your eye through the pupil is focused by the lens to form an image on your retina. But there is a spot on the retina, your blind spot, or *optic disk*, where nerves and blood vessels enter. Light that is focused on the blind spot cannot be seen. Find your own blind spot by making a black pencil mark the size of a dime on your paper. Make a small star about 3" to the right.

KEEP YOUR FACE 6" TO 8" AWAY FROM COINS

WHICH COINS DISAPPEAR?

HOLD PAPER 1 FOOT AWAY

Hold your paper about a foot away and stare at the star with your left eye and shut the right. Move the paper slowly toward you, and then back. When does the dime disappear? Or you can put 7 coins in a row on a table. Put your face 6" to 8" away and stare at the center coin. Close your left eye. Which coins seem to disappear? Now, try the other eye.

5 You can get an idea of what your blind spot and the tiny blood vessels in your retina "look" like. Shut one eye and touch the tip of a lighted penlight to the upper eyelid. Keep the tip moving gently in a tiny circle. What sensation do you get? Which part of your eyelid gives the best results? What happens when you stop moving the light?

6 Your retina has *photo-toreceptor* (light receiving) cells, which respond to incoming light. *Cones* are cells that are especially sensitive to bright light and colors. Cones are more numerous near the center of the retina. *Rod* photoreceptor

cells are scattered all over the retina, but especially *away* from the center. Rods are very sensitive to dim light and help you to see at night. Here's one way you can test how rod cells work.

Stand behind a friend who is looking straight ahead. Slowly and quietly move a pen or any small object from about 2 feet behind the head in a circle around to the front. Ask your friend to say "Stop!" as soon as he or she first can tell anything is there. Gradually bring the object forward. When can your friend see black and white? Colors? Identify the object? How good is your *peripheral* (side) vision?

STOP!

CRAYON OR ANY OTHER OBJECT

CLOSE ONE EYE AND TRY TO TOUCH PENCILS

TRY TO FOCUS ON FAR END OF STRAW

7 Hold a pen or pencil in each hand and at arm's length. Relax and bend your elbows just a bit. Close one eye and try to touch the two pencil points together. Now try it with both eyes open. Which way works best? How good is your *depth perception?* Next, put one end of a soda straw on the tip of your nose and point it away from you. Try to focus on the far end of the straw. How many straws do you see?

8 Images don't disappear right away after you're finished looking at something. Sometimes, one image is still causing a sensation (hanging in) and another image is placed on top of it. You

may have seen a Western movie where the wheels on a wagon seemed to be going backward. Here's how you can get that effect.

Color a 4″ circle of white cardboard with black, as shown above. Fasten your pinwheel onto the end of a pencil eraser with a thumbtack. Turn on your TV and spin your pinwheel in front of the screen as you watch the spokes. What do you see?

9 The black-and-white pinwheel gave you black and white *after-images.* You can also have after-images in color. Try this. Draw an American flag on a 4″ × 6″ piece of white paper or cardboard. Color the flag so there are 7 *green* stripes alternating with 6 *black* stripes and 50 *black* stars on an *orange* rectangle. Stare at your flag for 30 seconds or more while shining some extra light on it. Then quickly stare at a blank, light-colored wall or big piece of white paper. What happens? How long does the sensation last?

AFTERWORDS

Who makes a living by causing our eyes to play tricks on us? Magicians do! They use nimble fingers and distractions to lead us into seeing what isn't there. To help you understand how this "magic" works, try a trick with your friends.

First, be sure to wear a shirt or sweater and have a 25¢ coin ready. Then bend your left elbow and rest your fingertips on your right shoulder, near your collar. (Your elbow should be pointing down.) Tell the audience that you'll make the quarter disappear by rubbing it into your elbow.

Put the three middle fingers of your right hand together and lay the coin across the tips of them. Warn your audience that they should keep their eyes *on the quarter.* Then rub it in an up-and-down motion on the surface of your elbow. *Deliberately* let the quarter slip and fall to the floor. Pick it up in your *right* fingers and begin rubbing your elbow once again. Let the quarter drop at least two more times. By then your friends may call you clumsy—but agree with them.

Now suppose you have dropped the coin for the third time. This last time, quickly retrieve the coin with your *left* hand (even though all along you have been picking it up with your right). But keep the three fingers of your right hand close together as always.

Once you pick the coin up in your left hand, bend your arm back to your shoulder and slip the coin in the collar of your shirt or sweater. *At the same time,* take the three right-hand fingers and rub them on your elbow as before. When the quarter is safely tucked into your collar, throw both your hands forward, open your fingers, and yell "Presto!" Well, you warned your audience to keep their eyes on the quarter! Anyone who did should have caught the trick. But most people will be distracted by the dropping coin and won't notice that you switched the pick-up hand. That's magic!

Other magic tricks need special equipment or "props" to help create an illusion. Illusionists are magicians who work on a stage, farther away from a large audience. In these stunts, people may be made to "disappear" or be "changed" into other people or animals. (Did you think the lady in the box was really cut in half at the last magic show you saw?)

Natural illusions, such as *mirages,* can also occur— usually in wide, open spaces like deserts and oceans. For a mirage to happen, a layer of warm air must be sandwiched between two layers of cooler air. Light is refracted (bent) each time it enters or leaves one of these layers. This refraction can create the illusion of lakes and trees—even a whole city! The "lake" may even appear to have waves rippling across its surface. This is caused by the shifting of the different layers of air.

Since mirages are made by actual rays of light, it is possible for several people to see the same mirage. In fact, mirages can be photographed. So the next hot summer day, keep your eyes open for mirages—like the "puddles" you see ahead of you when you are riding on the highway. Don't let your eyes trick you into trying to splash around in one!

SECRET SIGNALS

SECRET SIGNALS

3 in x 5 in = 7.6 cm x 12.7 cm
1/4 in = .64 cm   15 ft = 4.6 m
2 in = 5.1 cm   30 ft = 9.1 m
1 ft = .3 m   300 mi = 483 km

Make a Secret Signal light to let you know when someone's coming near your room! It will take about one hour to build the light and set it up.

YOU WILL NEED

Standard flashlight that takes "D" batteries
2 "D" batteries
30 Feet of bell wire
Wide adhesive tape, duct tape, or other heavy-duty tape
2 Empty aluminum foil containers from frozen dinners, or 2 aluminum foil pie pans
Several large, thick rubber bands
Scissors, pliers
4 or 5 Pieces of paper, about 3" x 5" each

The electricity in your house runs on 120 volts, which is much too dangerous to handle. *Don't ever play around with it.* But you can find out how the electrical circuits in your house work by wiring your own Secret Signal light, which will light up when someone steps on the switch!

1 Decide where you are going to put the switch that will turn on your secret signal light. You could hide it under a rug or mat just outside the door to your room. Once you've decided where to put the switch, measure from that point to the place where you will put the light, and multiply by two. That's how many feet of bell wire you will need. **Note:** Don't try to put the switch more than 15 feet from the light, because the batteries are not strong enough to carry the electricity any farther than that.

2 Cut two pieces of bell wire, each one long enough to stretch from the switch to the light. (But include an extra foot or two of wire to be on the safe side.) Strip about 2" of plastic insulation away from the ends of both pieces of wire, exposing the bare copper wire inside. To do this, use the scissors to cut through the plastic, applying a *very gentle* pressure so that you won't cut all the way

A. CUT THRU THE PLASTIC COVERING ONLY!

through the wire. (You might make the first cut as a guide, then rotate the scissors so that the sharp edges cut only the plastic. See illustration **A**.)

3 Take the flashlight apart. You'll see that, at the light bulb end, there's a metal socket holding the bulb. Wrap one piece of wire around the end of the light bulb, making sure that the copper wire touches the metal socket. (See **B**.)

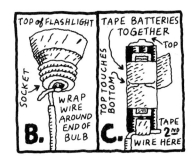

B. TOP OF FLASHLIGHT — SOCKET — WRAP WIRE AROUND END OF BULB

C. TAPE BATTERIES TOGETHER — TOP TOUCHES BOTTOM? — TOP — TAPE 2ND WIRE HERE

4 Use a wide piece of heavy-duty tape to tape the 2 "D" batteries together as shown in **C**. Wrap the tape *around* the sides of the batteries, but leave the ends of the batteries clear. Be sure the top (positive end) of one battery is touching the bottom (negative end) of the other. Next, tape the second copper wire to the bottom of the battery stack. Then put the batteries together with the top of the flashlight so that the nub on top of the battery touches the end of the light bulb. Tape the batteries to the top of the flashlight by running long pieces of tape down one side, across the bottom, and up the other side of the whole thing. What you've done is to rebuild the flashlight *without* the long part of the outside case.

5 Now you should be able to make the light bulb light up by touching the ends of the two dangling wires together. If it doesn't work, check to be sure your

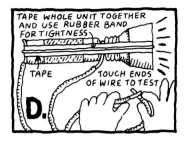

TAPE WHOLE UNIT TOGETHER AND USE RUBBER BAND FOR TIGHTNESS

TAPE

TOUCH ENDS OF WIRE TO TEST

D.

connections are tight. Is the first wire still touching the metal socket around the bulb? Is the second wire pressed tightly against the bottom of the stack of batteries? Wrap one or more long, strong rubber bands around the whole thing to keep the batteries, wire, and light bulb pressed together tightly. (See **D**.)

6 Cut off the sides from two aluminum pie pans or frozen dinner pans, and throw the sides away. With the tip of your scissors, poke a small hole in each pie pan, about ¼" from the edge. Connect one pie pan to each of the dangling wires attached to the flashlight by putting the copper end of the wire through the hole and bending it around to make a loop. When both pie pans are connected, touch them together and the light will light up. This is your switch.

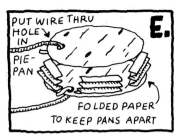

PUT WIRE THRU HOLE IN PIE-PAN

E.

FOLDED PAPER TO KEEP PANS APART

7 Fold over several 3" × 5" pieces of paper until you have strips of paper that are several thicknesses thick. Tape the thick paper strips to the top of one pie pan, around the edges. These strips are pad-

ding, which will keep the pie pans slightly separated. (See **E**.)

8 Now you're ready to hide the pie-pan switch under a rug near your door. Lift the rug and put the padded pie pan down with the paper strips facing up. Put the other pie pan on top of the first one, and replace the rug. The padding should keep the pie pans apart until you step on the rug on top of them. Then their middles will touch (where there's no padding), the circuit will be complete, and the light will light up! Put the light in your room, and tape the wires to the baseboard so they won't show.

YOUR SECRET SIGNAL

DAD STEPS DOWN

PANS ARE HIDDEN UNDER RUG

VARIATIONS

■ Use a dry-cell battery and a small light-bulb socket with two screw terminals on each side of the bulb. That way, you can actually twist the wires around the screws, and the connections won't come loose.

■ Be a scientist and invent a way to set up a signal light that will come on when you open a drawer or closet door.

■ When you're done using the Secret Signals light, find out how the length of the wire affects the brightness of the bulb. Cut the wires attached to the pie pan switch in half, and strip away the plastic coating. Touch the copper ends together. Is the bulb brighter now? Cut the wires again so that they're only 1 foot long. Why do you think the bulb gets brighter when the wires are shorter?

AFTERWORDS

In Secret Signals you made a *circuit,* a complete circle of wire and/or other substances that would conduct electricity. You saw that if the circuit was broken, the electricity didn't flow. Electricity must *always* flow in an unbroken circle, always returning to its point of origin; that's a primary characteristic of electrical current. To understand why, you have to understand just what makes an electrical current.

The copper atoms in a piece of wire all have the same number of protons, neutrons, and electrons, and this number must always remain the same. It's kind of like the number of seats on a bus. There are only so many seats, and if you have a rule that no one is allowed to stand on the bus, then the bus can only hold a certain number of people. With atoms, you can't add a few extra protons or electrons — the atomic structure has no extra "seats" for them. Besides that, atoms have a rule that says the bus must always be full: If one of the protons, neutrons, or electrons wants to get off the bus, another of the same kind has to get on.

For now, don't worry about the protons and neutrons; they can't move from one atom, or bus, to the next. But the *electrons* in copper can. However, if one electron moves from, let's say, the first bus and gets on the second one, then an electron from the second bus must get off to make room for it — to keep the number of electrons constant. So the electron from the second bus moves to the third one, causing an electron to move from the third bus to the fourth, and so on. This flow of electrons from one atom to another is an electric current.

But this chain reaction can't occur unless there is a circular route, a circuit, for the electrons to take, so that the last atom can pass its "extra" electron back to the first one. Remember, the first atom gave up one of its electrons to start this whole process going. Because the laws of nature say that each atom must always maintain the same number of electrons, the first atom in line must get an electron back. As long as the atoms are arranged in a circular path, the electrons can keep moving from one atom to another.

What if the circular path for electricity was made out of saltwater taffy instead of copper wire? Would the electrons in taffy jump from one to another? No, because taffy isn't a *conductor.* A conductor is any material in which the electrons can move freely from one atom to another. Metals — especially copper and aluminum — are good conductors because their electrons are free to move around. But the electrons in taffy can't, so taffy is called an *insulator.* (But plastic is most commonly used to insulate copper wire.)

This simple example of circuitry extends all the way to the power plant that supplies electricity to your city or town. Even when the power plant is 300 miles from your home, the current must make the trip back to its source to complete the circuit. That's why you always see *two* wires running along the telephone and power poles at the roadside. One wire sends the current out across the countryside. The other wire is the "return" wire, which allows the current to go "home."

A MATTER OF TASTE

A MATTER OF TASTE

1 tsp = 5 ml
2 tsp = 10 ml

Most people love to eat! Part of the fun in eating depends on how food tastes. Can you imagine a hot dog without mustard or relish? Boring! These taste treats should take about an hour.

EXPERIMENT No. 1: MAPPING YOUR TONGUE

All of our tastes can be put into 4 main groups: *sweet* (sugar or honey or molasses), *sour* (lemons or limes or vinegar), *salty* (table salt) and *bitter* (baking chocolate or instant coffee). Your taste-tester — your tongue — can be grouped into 4 parts, too. Here's how.

YOU WILL NEED
Salt
Sugar
Vinegar
Instant coffee
Large paper cups
Small paper cups
Cotton swabs (Q-Tips)
Paper and pencil
Mirror
Blindfold (handkerchief or scarf)

1 Look in a mirror and stick out your tongue. Make a sketch of your tongue that looks like this. Make it about as big as the palm of your hand.

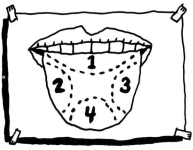

2 You will need separate solutions of salt, sugar, vinegar, and instant coffee. Put 2 level teaspoons of each substance into half a cup of water and stir. These are your "stock solutions"; label them. Next, label 4 smaller cups and pour a teaspoon of each stock solution into the proper cup. Put a cotton swab in each cup.

3 Blindfold a friend and tell him/her to stick out his/her tongue. Then take the swab out of one of the smaller cups, but don't tell your friend which one. Gently touch this swab to your friend's tongue in region 1. What does your friend taste when the swab first touches the tongue: sweet, like sugar; sour, like vinegar; salty, like table salt, or bitter, like coffee?

4 Record your friend's answer by writing one of the following symbols on your sketch of a tongue: "SW" for sweet; "SR" for sour; "SA" for salty; and "B" for bitter.

5 Do the same thing on regions 2, 3, and 4 (in that order). Then have your friend rinse the mouth with clean water and spit it out into another big paper cup. Repeat step 3 for each of the other 3 solutions.

6 Repeat testing all 4 solutions at least one more time, but the more times the better. Test other people, but be sure to use clean cups and swabs for each subject you test. Which parts of the tongue seem to be best for tasting each of the 4 tastes? How much do the taste regions overlap?

EXPERIMENT No. 2: NAME THAT TASTE

Now use your trusty tongue to see if it can identify different kinds of foods — even if you can't see or smell them!

YOU WILL NEED

Some different hard fruits and vegetables (such as potato, pear, apple, carrot, onion, squash, radish, turnip, parsnip, rutabaga, broccoli stem, cauliflower stem, sweet potato, or whatever other foods like these you have at home)
Paring knife
Paper cups
Toothpicks
Blindfold

1 Peel each of the fruits and vegetables, and cut them up into little pieces about the size of the eraser on a pencil. Put each food in a separate cup and label the cup.

2 Blindfold your friend and tell him/her to pinch his/her nose shut. Then use a clean toothpick to feed your friend a small piece of one of the foods. What does your friend think the food is?

3 Keep a record of your friend's guess by writing down the name of the food and putting a + beside it if he/she gets it right. (You may want to write down what he/she *thought* it was, if they don't guess right.)

4 Have your friend rinse his/her mouth with clear water between tests of each of the foods, so there's no leftover taste on the tongue. How many foods did your friend guess correctly?

5 Repeat steps 2, 3, and 4, but this time don't have the nose pinched shut. How many did your friend guess correctly this time? How does your sense of smell affect your sense of taste? Repeat all steps with another friend, but don't forget to use a clean toothpick with your next customer.

VARIATIONS

■ Try feeding your blind-folded partner a piece of apple while you hold a piece of pear (or onion) close under his/her nose. What does he/she think is being eaten?

■ Suck an ice cube for a few minutes. How do things taste when your tongue is cold?

■ Pinch a copper penny, sandwiched by a small piece of aluminum foil, between your thumb and first finger. Touch the free ends of the two metals (the edge where the foil was cut) to the tip of your tongue. How does it taste?

■ How well can you tell the taste of sugar solution from artificial sweeteners? (Try the regular brand of some pop and the diet brand of the same pop.) Which one do ants and flies go for?

■ Repeat Experiment No. 2 but this time don't use a blind-fold or pinch your nose. Put some potato in a blender, add some green food coloring (Happy St. Patrick's Day?), and mix well. Do the same with other light-colored foods, like pear, apple, radish, turnip. How does color affect your sense of taste? Your enjoy-ment of food?

AFTERWORDS

What does rotten meat have to do with the discovery of America? Well, back in the time of Columbus there were no refrigerators, so fresh meat spoiled very quickly and smelled and tasted "bad." But even spoiled meat was too valuable to throw away, so people started to add spices and herbs to hide the rotten taste. These seasonings had to be brought from the Far East and Africa and this made them expensive. Columbus was looking for a quick way to the Far East when he bumped into America.

How do you like your chili? Hot? The sense of taste varies from person to person. Stick out your tongue and look at it in the mirror. You will see bumps and ridges be-tween them. Within these bumps there are thousands of tiny *taste buds*. These are specialized cells connected by sensory nerves to your brain. When chemicals (food) are dissolved in the liquid on the surface of your tongue, they stimulate the taste buds and the nerves carry the mes-sage to the brain. Your brain then lets you know what you are tasting. There are 4 kinds of taste cells, one for each of the main tastes. Taste buds for sweet things are mostly located at the tip of your tongue. You taste most bitter things with taste buds at the back of your tongue. Sour and salty things are mostly picked up by taste buds on the edges of your tongue.

If you touch a penny or a piece of aluminum foil to your tongue, you feel a taste that is not caused by food. In this case, your taste buds are electrically stimulated by a *weak* electric current that is produced by the two differ-ent metals and your saliva. (Don't try this with any other kinds of electricity!)

How do things taste when your nose is stuffed up with a cold? Much of what we taste has to do with our sense of smell. In great-grand-mother's time a favorite medi-cine was Castor Oil. It smelled rotten. Whenever she gave some to a child, she would pinch the child's nose shut. How good an idea was this? What part of your tongue should you avoid if you ever have to take bitter medicine?

You can tell right away if a food is too salty. But you may find that a piece of lemon doesn't taste sour until you actually bite down on it and some juice comes out. How well and how quickly you can taste something depends upon how well it dissolves in the liquid on your tongue. Salt dissolves very quickly. Solid lemon does not dissolve as quickly as lemon juice.

How do you like your pizza, hot or cold? Most peo-ple prefer hot foods because they seem to taste better. For one thing, hot foods give off more odors, which help to pep up your sense of taste. Warm foods also help to stim-ulate your taste buds. What happens to your sense of taste after you suck on an ice cube for a while?

Long ago, rich people and rulers, like kings and queens, were afraid that someone might try to poison them, so they would hire "official tasters" to sample food before it was eaten. Even today there are professional "tasters" who taste various blends of tea or wines to get the "blend" of several different tea leaves or wine grapes just right. What a tasty way to make a living!

MARBLEIZED PAPER

MARBLEIZED PAPER

How would you like to make wrapping paper that looks like real marble, with swirls of color? You don't have to be a great artist. Just put science to work for you and in about 30 minutes you can create a work of art.

YOU WILL NEED

3 Drinking glasses
Water
Small amounts of assorted beverages (milk, juices, soft drinks) and household liquids (vinegar, detergents)
Teaspoon
Salt
Vegetable oil
Food coloring
Newspapers
A large rectangular baking dish, tray, dishpan, or disposable aluminum roasting pan, big enough to hold the paper
Hobby paints: *oil-based,* in various colors (available in small square jars wherever model airplanes are sold)
Stick or paint stirrer
White notepaper and sheets of paper large enough to be used as gift wrap (pads of artist's "layout bond" work well)
Dishwashing liquid
Salad oil or turpentine or paint thinner for clean-up
Paper towels

Maybe you've heard that oil and water don't mix. But are there other liquids that won't mix with water? Is there a way to *force* oil and water to mix? When you find out the answers to those questions, you'll understand why marbleized paper is easy to make.

1 Fill a drinking glass half full of water and add a small amount of milk. Stir. Do the two liquids mix together or do they separate? Rinse out the glass and try the experiment with other beverages. Do all liquids mix with water? Can you find a liquid in your kitchen that will *not* mix with water? **CAUTION:** DO NOT DRINK THE EXPERIMENTS!

2 Clean the glasses and begin again. Fill one glass with cold water and one glass with hot water. At the same time, add a teaspoon of salt to each glass and stir. Which glass of water dissolves the salt faster? Pour ½ cup of vegetable oil into the third glass, add a teaspoon of salt, and stir. What happens?

3 Find out whether or not you can *make* oil and water mix! Start with a clean glass, filled halfway with water. Add a few drops of food coloring, so you'll be able to tell the water from the oil more easily. Now add a few teaspoonfuls of vegetable oil and stir madly! If you stir fast enough, will the oil and water finally mix? Does the food coloring mix better with the oil or water?

4 Now it's time to take advantage of the Great Oil and Water Feud and make beautiful marbleized paper! Spread newspapers on the floor near your workspace to use as a drying area. Fill your flat baking dish, tray, or disposable roasting pan half full of water. Add a small amount of hobby paint to the water. See how it floats on the surface? Use a stick to swirl

the paint around. You can marbleize your paper now, or add more colors first. When the floating paints look good to you, lay the paper on the surface of the water for a few seconds. (Until you get the hang of it, experiment with the small notepaper before you go on to the larger paper.) Work quickly and don't soak the paper. That way it won't wrinkle. Lift it off and look at your designs! You'll probably be able to marbleize one or two more sheets of paper before you need to add more paint. Experiment with stirring

the water rapidly and then quickly putting the paper on the surface while the paint and water are still moving.

5 Find our how soap affects the oil-and-water combination by adding a squirt of dishwashing liquid to the mixture. What happens if you add the soap without stirring the paint and water? What happens if you stir it up first? Can you get different marbleized effects this way?

6 Let your marbleized paper dry, paint-side up, on newspapers for several hours before using it. If the paper is slightly wrinkled, you can iron it between two sheets of plain paper. Use a low setting on your iron.

7 Clean your marbleizing tray and utensils with salad oil or paint thinner.

VARIATIONS

■ You can marbleize vases, cardboard and plastic boxes, pencils, and other objects that have a smooth, solid-color surface. Boxes can be marbleized in the tray by simply laying the box on the surface of the water, one side at a time. For other objects, use a bucket of water instead of a tray, and

get the water moving before you dip the object.

■ Create special designs by swirling a marbleizing "comb" through the floating paints. You can make the comb yourself: Use a strip of heavy cardboard about 1" wide and 8" long; push some pins through the cardboard in a straight row, spaced ½ inch apart. Or use toothpicks stuck into a piece of Styrofoam.

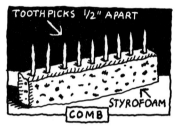

■ To make marbleized note cards and envelopes, use sheets of stationery folded in half. If you dip the envelopes, don't use too much paint and be sure to keep the gummed flaps *dry.* You can write on your marbleized paper if the paint isn't too thick.

■ Make book covers from your marbleized paper. Or better yet, "publish" your own book and paste the marbleized paper on the inside of the front and back covers. That's the way it's done for special editions of handmade books.

AFTERWORDS

Marbleized paper was created in Persia 400 years ago, and it has been made just about the same way ever since. In France, England, Italy, and, later, in the United States, beautiful marbleized papers were often used as endpapers: the decorative papers that are pasted down on the *inside* front and back covers of books. For an example, you might check your local public library and/or school library. If they have old copies of Webster's New International Dictionary, Second Edition, the endpapers will probably be marbleized paper.

Other old books in your library might have a variation of marbleized paper: marbled edges. Even as recently as the 1950s, apprentice bookbinders were taught how to marbleize book edges by hand. The pages of the book were held tightly together in a clamp, and then dipped quickly into the multicolored paints floating on the surface in a vat of water. Master bookbinders knew how to use combs and rakes to create specific standard patterns with names like Peacock and Agate.

Today marbleized endpapers and edges are rarely used, but when they do appear, they are still made by hand, and still use the principle that oil and water won't mix. But water mixes well with most other substances. In fact, water can dissolve so many substances that chemists call it a *universal solvent*. The substance a solvent dissolves is called the *solute,* and the mixture that results is called a *solution.*

Your kitchen is full of solutions that you drink every day. Lemonade, coffee, tea, apple juice, and soft drinks are all solutions with one or more solutes dissolved in them. Have you ever noticed that sugar dissolves more easily in hot tea than in iced tea? That's because the *solubility* of a solid—in other words, the ability of a solid to dissolve—increases when the temperature of the solvent goes up.

But here's a surprise: The opposite is true when the solute is a *gas*. With gases, the colder the solvent, the more soluble the gas is. Maybe you didn't even know that gases could be dissolved! Well, they can—and that's how soft drinks are made. The gas *carbon dioxide* is actually dissolved in water, along with sugar and some other flavors, to make the fizzy carbonated drinks people love. Now that you know how temperature affects the solubility of gases, you can understand why sodas left out in warm weather always taste flat!

One beverage you'll find in your refrigerator isn't a solution at all. Scientists call milk a *colloid,* rather than a solution, because there is something in milk that can't be dissolved. Can you guess what it is? It's the butterfat, of course! Fifty years ago, before milk was homogenized, the cream—which has most of the butterfat—would separate from the milk and rise to the top of the bottle. (That was in the days when milk came in bottles.) Though cream looks thicker and "heavier" than milk, the tiny particles of fat in cream are lighter than the rest of the milk.

Today, however, the butterfat never separates from the milk because homogenization is standard in the United States. During this milk-processing method, the small particles of butterfat are forced through a valve and made even smaller. Once the butterfat particles are the right size, they neither rise nor sink, because they aren't lighter or heavier than the rest of the milk.

So next time you sip a glass of milk, you can say thanks to technology for the homogenization that gives you a smoother drink. But when it comes to making marbleized paper, there is no need for technological tricks. The natural conflict between oil and water brings about a more beautiful creation.

1/2 in = 1.27 cm
1 in = 2.54 cm
8 in = 20.3 cm
1/2 C = .12 l
1 tsp = 5 ml

BRINY BEHAVIOR

BRINY BEHAVIOR

1/2 in = 1.27 cm
1 in = 2.54 cm
150° F= 65° C
1/2 C = .12 l

How would you like to have an animal laboratory full of sea monkeys? That's what brine shrimp are sometimes called. You can raise dozens of brine shrimp in a small jar or bowl—and then experiment with them to find out what they like, and *don't* like! The raising will take a few days, and the testing, a few minutes.

Shrimp Farming
YOU WILL NEED

2 Clean wide-mouth jars or
    large drinking glasses
Vial of brine-shrimp eggs
    (you can find these at
    a pet shop)
Magnifying glass
Ruler and pencil
Few tablespoons of coarse
    sea salt (found in grocery
    or health-food stores)
Measuring spoon and cup
Masking tape
1 Package dry yeast
Note: You will also need all of the things listed under "Shrimp Testing."

1 Fill 2 clean jars or large drinking glasses with tap water and let them stand, uncovered, for at least 24 hours to rid the water of any chlorine. Use this water in all of your experiments.
Do not use metal containers!

2 Take a close look at your brine-shrimp eggs under a magnifying glass. What shape are they? How many of them could sit side by side on a line 1" long? Add about one level tablespoon of sea salt to a cup of your standing water and stir until dissolved. This will make the salty water called brine. Pour the brine into a clean glass jar and mark the level of the liquid with masking tape. Bigger jars may need more cups of brine. Sprinkle a pinch of brine-shrimp eggs on the surface of the brine. Set the jar in a warm place—such as a sunny spot on the kitchen counter. You will have to check your jars every day and add more brine up to the tape mark, as needed.

3 Watch your container carefully and often during the next two days. Hold your container up to the light and use a magnifying glass to see what's happening. The new shrimp will be very tiny—almost invisible! Look for tiny white dots swimming wildly in the water.

If you don't see any new shrimp within 3 days, something has gone wrong. Start again, this time using different amounts of salt in your brine. Or try different water, such as distilled water. Or use pond water filtered through a paper towel. If you still don't hatch any shrimp, you might need a new batch of eggs—a new brand, if possible.

4 Once you see shrimp, sprinkle a few (*very* few!) grains of powdered dry yeast on the surface of the water every couple of days. If the water stays milky after a while, you are giving them too much food.

HOW MANY SHRIMP COULD YOU FIT SIDE BY SIDE?

SCHOOL RULER

PICK A SUNNY SPOT ON KITCHEN COUNTER FOR JAR

MARK THE LEVEL OF LIQUID WITH TAPE

SALT

5 Each day, spend some time studying your brine shrimp. How do they change as they grow? Females are usually larger than males. How else can you tell them apart? Watch for eggs and "babies." But don't expect your shrimp to get too big. Even the biggest "adult" shrimp are only about ½" long. In your laboratory, they may not even grow up to be *that* big.

Now that your shrimp are growing well, you can either keep them as pets (in which case you have to name *all* of them!) or you can turn your collection of brine shrimp into an animal laboratory, and put your shrimp to the test!

Shrimp Testing
YOU WILL NEED
Plastic spoon
Tall, narrow jar or glass
Construction paper or brown paper bag
Rubber band
Flashlight
Rectangular glass baking dish
Red and blue cellophane
Ice cube
Sandwich bag
Small cup
Red food coloring

1 Test to see how your shrimp react to light. If the brine shrimp are already in a tall glass, great! If not, use a plastic spoon to move some of them to a clean, tall glass or bottle filled with brine. Wrap construction paper or several layers of brown paper around the outside of the glass. Hold the paper in place with a rubber band. Shine a flashlight directly down onto the surface of the brine for 3 minutes. While holding the light in place, quickly remove the paper. Where are most of the shrimp? Can you tell what direction they are swimming in?

2 Pour a jar of your shrimp-and-brine mixture into a flat glass baking dish. Stretch red cellophane over one half of the dish and blue over the other half. Watch for a while. Do the shrimp seem to prefer one end of the dish? Can you guess why?

3 See how well your brine shrimp can take the cold. Seal an ice cube inside a plastic sandwich bag and put it in the brine, at one end of the baking dish. Watch for a few minutes. How do your shrimp react? Remove the ice cube. Then repeat the experiment—but put hot water in the plastic bag instead of ice.

RED FOOD COLORING AND YEAST IN 1/2 CUP OF BRINE

ICE CUBE IN PLASTIC BAG

COVER DISH WITH RED CELLOPHANE AND BLUE CELLOPHANE

SHINE FLASHLIGHT DIRECTLY DOWN INTO GLASS

WRAP BROWN PAPER AROUND TALL GLASS FILLED WITH BRINE

RED FOOD COLORING

ST/87

4 Put some shrimp eggs in the freezer for a day or so. Will they still hatch, after they've been frozen? Put a different batch of eggs in an oven for a few hours at 150 degrees. Can you still get these to hatch when you take them out of the oven?

5 With a plastic spoon, put a few shrimp into a separate cup half full of brine. Mix a drop of red food coloring with a small pinch of yeast, and gently add the red yeast to the cup. After 5 to 10 minutes, spoon out some of the shrimp. What do you see? If the shrimp have eaten the red yeast, you should be able to see their digestive systems.

AFTERWORDS

Now that you've done so many different experiments on the brine shrimp in your animal laboratory, it's time to play that great game show — *The $15,000 Brine Shrimp Fortune Quiz!* For all the money and a trip to Salt Lake City, Utah, answer this question: Where do brine shrimp come from — the ocean, the forest, or the desert?

Believe it or not, the answer is the desert. Brine shrimp are found in America in the dry areas of the Southwest, where there is little rainfall and many lakes dry up for much of the year. When rain does fall, it fills the lakes again and also forms puddles. Brineshrimp eggs hatch in these salty lakes and puddles, and live until the hot sun evaporates the water completely. Then the next batch of brineshrimp eggs, which were laid while the shrimp were alive, pile up on the desert and wait for the rains to come again.

Brine shrimp are *crustaceans* — like lobsters, crayfish, and crabs. So naturally you're wondering: How did brine shrimp get out of the ocean and find their way to Utah? Actually, although brine shrimp are in the same class with lobsters, they are not really descended from shellfish and they never did live in the ocean. Instead, brine shrimp evolved from other freshwater crustaceans. They've been inland for thousands and thousands of years.

In your briny behavior experiments, you tricked your brine shrimp into thinking there was a lot of food around when there wasn't! Brine shrimp are attracted to areas with lots of green algae, because that's what shrimp eat. Green algae absorb most of the blue light in the sun's spectrum, and that leaves mainly red light shining on the shrimp. By putting red-colored cellophane over the brine shrimp, you were able to trick them into thinking that the water was full of algae. That's a pretty good trick — much easier than having to come up with a pan full of algae!

But what happens to the eggs if the weather is very dry and hot for a very long time? When you checked out the briny behavior of your tiny shrimp, you probably found out that the eggs *will* hatch, even if they've been baked in the oven for a few hours. And they will hatch even if they've been frozen. Brine-shrimp eggs are amazingly resistant to the destructive forces in nature, because desert temperatures are often blistering at noon in summer and freezing at night in winter. Sometimes brine-shrimp eggs will sit around on the desert for

2 or 3 years before the conditions are right for them to hatch.

The Great Salt Lake in Utah is another main residence for brine shrimp, but there the life cycle is not interrupted by these long drying-out spells. Many of the brine-shrimp eggs you find in pet stores come from the Great Salt Lake. People buy these brine-shrimp eggs to raise them for food for their tropical fish, because tropical fish grow more quickly when they're fed live food.

But who eats brine shrimp in nature? Nobody. Not many other creatures live in the salty puddles and lakes. In the Great Salt Lake, there are only two kinds of flies, one species of insect, and some algae floating around — so the brine shrimp pretty much have the run of the place.

GOOD LOOKER

GOOD LOOKER

With a periscope, you can peek around corners without being seen! It will take less than an hour to make and decorate one Good Looker.

YOU WILL NEED

Empty box from aluminum foil, plastic wrap, or waxed paper
Masking tape
Utility knife or paring knife
2 Small mirrors about 2" × 3" (available at Woolworth's and other variety stores)
White glue (Elmer's Glue-All or similar brand)
Colored paper, paints, markers

Everyone knows what you see when you look into a mirror. You see yourself. But what happens when you look into two mirrors? If they're set up right, you can see over and around things that are blocking your view. That's how tanks and submarines get a good look at the world outside and above them. They use mirrors, mounted inside a long tube. Whether you call that tube a periscope or a Good Looker, it's a great toy and a lot of fun to use!

1 Cover the sharp, serrated edge of an empty aluminum foil or plastic wrap box with one or two layers of masking tape. This will keep you from cutting yourself on the edge while you work.

2 Use a utility knife or sharp paring knife to cut a window in the front side of the box, at one end of it. The window should be about 1½" inches long, and almost as wide as the box. *Be careful with the knife.* This might be a good time for parents to show children how to use one. Cut another window of the same size in the *back side* of the box, at the *opposite* end.

3 Put one of the mirrors on its edge in the box, so that it faces the first window at about a 45-degree angle. One end of the mirror should be wedged into the corner nearest the window. The other end of the mirror should be taped to the back

side of the box. Don't worry if the angle isn't *exactly* 45 degrees, because the size of the box will determine what angle you use. Place the other mirror parallel to the first one in a similar position at the other end of the box. (See the diagram.)

4 Tape the mirrors in place and close the box. Look through one window to see if your periscope is working. If it is, open the box and glue the mirrors permanently in place by running a thin line of white glue along each edge of each mirror. If the periscope isn't working, adjust the position of the mirrors. *Make sure the*

mirrors are parallel and that they are facing into the middle — not the corners — of the box.

5 When the glue has dried and you're sure the mirrors won't move, close the lid of the box again and glue or tape it shut.

6 Decorate the outside of your Good Looker, using colored paper, wrapping paper, stickers, markers, crayons, magazine cut outs, fabric scraps, or anything else you have on hand. If you're making this periscope as a gift for someone you know, why not put her name on it as part of the decoration?

■ What can you see with your Good Looker? Does it give you a good way to look at birds? What happens when you try to walk toward something you see in your periscope? What if you stick it out the window and try to look at the sky?

■ Perhaps an older person could use your periscope to see what's on top of the refrigerator…or on a shelf that's too high to reach… or to find out what's under the couch without bending over. Think of as many ways to use your periscope as you can!

VARIATIONS

Don't look now, but there are more things you can do with mirrors:

■ Set a small mirror at an angle in a shallow pan of water. Place the pan near a window so that a direct beam of sunlight hits the mirror. It will make rainbows on the wall.

MIRROR

■ To see yourself as others see you, hold two mirrors at right angles so that they form a corner or an L. Tape the mirrors together and set them on a table. Look into the corner,

where the two mirrors come together. Do you notice anything different about yourself? This is how you really look to other people. No matter how many times you've looked in a mirror, you've never seen the face that other people see — because the mirror image you usually see is backward.

Scratch your right ear, while looking into the L-shaped mirrors. Did your right ear seem to be on the wrong side? That's because you're actually looking at a mirror image of a mirror image! Try to point to a particular tooth…or your biggest freckle…or try to wipe a crumb from your face. It's not so easy! This double image is just one of the many deceptions of mirrors.

AFTERWORDS

Mirror, mirror on the wall — and in telescopes and cameras, in supermarket checkouts, in photocopying machines. In fact, just about everywhere you look you'll find mirrors being used in countless and surprising ways.

And which one is the fairest of them all? That's hard to say, but the *biggest* of them all is the mirror in the world's largest telescope on Mount Semirodriki in the U.S.S.R. It is 236.2 inches across — just 36.2 inches bigger than the Hale telescope on Mount Palomar in California. With instruments such as these, astronomers can see farther into space than they ever could before. Imagine sitting in the observer's cage in the middle of a gigantic steel tube, with your *back* to the sky. You're facing an astronomical mirror, as the light from the stars travels past you down the tube, and is reflected back to a spot just in front of you called the *prime focus*. Many people think that the lenses are responsible for the magnification provided by these enormous telescopes. But actually, except for the small eyepiece that pinpoints the prime focus, there are no lenses in these powerful reflecting telescopes. Instead, a single concave mirror gathers light from the stars and magnifies it *thousands* of times!

Unlike the concave mirrors used in telescopes, which are expensive and difficult to make, flat mirrors are fairly inexpensive and they are being used in industry in a variety of new, problem-solving ways. Mirrors are at work in the newest supermarkets and large drugstores. For several years now, laser-beam checkout systems have been used to read the Universal Product Code (UPC) prices — those vertical black lines you find on almost everything you buy. The checkout clerk passes the UPC markings over a laser scanner, and the product name and price are automatically rung up on the cash register.

But however mirrors are used, the principles of reflected light are all primarily the same. What happens with a flat mirror is this: Rays of light coming from an object in front of the mirror strike the mirror and bounce off at an angle that is equal to the original angle of light. For instance, let's say that you are in front of a small mirror at point A, and your friend is at point B. (See the illustration.) The light coming from you strikes the mirror at point C. If you drew an imaginary line perpendicular to the mirror at point C, then you could measure this angle, which is called the *incident angle.* Your friend can see you, because the light bounces *off* the mirror from C to B at an angle that is equal to the incident angle.

The interesting thing about these principles of reflected light is that when we look at reflections coming from a mirror, the light is *actually* coming from point C on the mirror. But the image appears to come from a point *behind* the mirror — point Z in the diagram. You can prove this with a camera that adjusts for distances. Stand 3 feet away from the mirror and set the camera focus for 3 feet. The picture you take will be blurry. Only if you focus the camera on the image of yourself *behind the mirror,* which is 6 feet away from where you are standing, will the picture be clear and sharp.

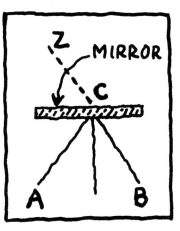

SUPER STRAWS

SUPER STRAWS

1/4 in = .64 cm	
1/2 in = 1.27 cm	
3/4 in = 1.9 cm	
1 in = 2.54 cm	
15 lbs = 6.8 kg	

Faster than a speeding bullet, more powerful than a locomotive, able to leap tall buildings in a single bound. It's a bird, it's a plane, it's Superstraw! *Superstraw?* Yes, that device **that** allows you to slurp soda can be used to defy gravity and support a thousand times its weight! It should take about 30 minutes to build these super straw structures.

YOU WILL NEED

1 Box of soda straws (*not* the flexible type)

A few large paper clips

1 Pound of 1" nails or marbles, or any objects of uniform size that can be counted

Roll of plastic or masking tape

6 Or more cardboard cups, or empty soup cans

1 Tube of hobby glue

Scissors

1 Box of straight pins

1 Raw potato

2 Scraps of wood (½" to ¾" thick) the same size as the sole of your foot

Gravity is pulling us downward all the time. But we're not alone. Gravity pulls *everything* on the Earth downward toward its center. Even air, although it is invisible, has weight and is a real substance, like a solid or a liquid, and is acted upon by the forces of gravity. As a matter of fact, there is about 15 pounds of air pressure on each square inch of surface at sea level! So why don't buildings collapse and bridges fall into the waters below them? Because we've learned how to deal with gravity. We know how to use the opposing forces that exert a push against gravity.

By using straws and a few other items, you can see how the forces of gravity work—in the miniature bridges you will build and then in the great spans of real bridges on which you ride or walk. Also, see how the lowly straw can disperse pressure and can hold up a weight many times its own.

Imagine one of the first,

most primitive bridges man ever encountered. It was probably a log fallen across a stream and over which one or two people could walk at a time. Today's bridges span great rivers and bays, often for many miles. These bridges hold tons of vehicles and passengers at one time, efficiently and safely. Yet, the basic principle is the same: The upward supporting forces must be greater than the downward pull of gravity.

1 Let's make a 1-log type of bridge by using 1 straw and see how much of a load it can carry. First, make supports by stacking up two piles of

HOW MANY NAILS DOES IT TAKE TO BEND THE STRAW?

books so the height of each pile is equal to the other. (You can also use two chairs placed almost together or two table surfaces.)

Slip the straw through the loop of the paper clip. Place the ends of the straw between two piles of books. Attach a paper cup to the clip (tape it, if necessary) and begin putting nails into it or wrap tape around soup can twice (near top rim) and then slip the paper clip through, for a hanger. How many nails does it take to bend the straw? How many to make the straw collapse? Use extra paper clips and cups, if needed.

Move the two book piles, first closer together and then farther apart, and again see how many nails it takes to collapse the straw in each of those positions. What difference does the distance between supports make in how much load the straw can carry?

2 Tape another soda straw to the first one with the paper clip. You've made a *beam*. Suspend this between the two book piles. Again, hang the paper clip and paper cup from the beam. Add nails to the cup.

How many nails does it take to make the beam collapse? Does the double straw or beam construction carry more or less than twice the load of a single straw?

3 Build a beam with three straws this way: Place one straw *on top* of the other two so that

when viewed from one end, a triangle is formed. Tape them together.

Suspend the paper clip

TAPE 3 STRAWS FOR A TRIANGULAR BEAM

and cup and determine how much of a load this will carry.

Build another triangular beam, but this time *glue* the three straws together as well as taping them. Let dry and again determine how strong this one is. This is called a *laminated beam*.

4 Make your own Great Bridge: Place the two piles of books 1 straw-length PLUS another ½ straw-length apart. Use straws, tape, glue, scissors and even straight pins to make a strong bridge that will span the

distance between the two book piles. You might want to connect soda straws by sliding one inside the other. Remember also the strength in the triangular beam.

What is the greatest load it can carry before collapsing? Use the nails and cups and/or the metal food cans to find out.

5 Build a small, strong bridge with as few straws, glue, and tape as necessary, but one that can still support a heavy book. Place the two piles of books 1½ straw-lengths apart. Which bridge formation supported the book's weight?

6 Have you ever tried to push a straw through a raw potato? It is almost impossible, isn't it? But if you take that same straw and hold one index finger over one end of the straw and jab the potato with one swift stab of the other end of the straw, it will sink right into the potato. Surprised? It worked because, by holding your finger over the end of the straw, you trapped the air inside and the pressure was concentrated in the straw.

With all that pressure on one point, the straw took on a stronger force. Now let's use this same pressure idea, but let's spread it around.

Would you believe that a single straw can support your body's weight? Try this: Use sharp scissors to cut a straw into small pieces, each about ¼" long. Make each piece the same length. Glue these pieces upright on a piece of wood about as big as the sole of your shoe. Try to space them equal distances apart and let the glue harden. Lay another piece of wood about the same size over the tops of the straw pieces. Put one foot on top of the upper board and gently shift all of your weight onto the board. Have someone look between the boards. Do the straws collapse? How much weight can the straw pieces support if you put them closer together? Get more pieces to do this. How much weight can the straw pieces support if you make them longer? Shorter?

AFTERWORDS

Just as your skeletal system (along with your muscular system, of course) holds you up, the skeletal system of a structure such as a bridge keeps IT up. Any bridge or structure you see has two kinds of forces acting upon it. One force, *gravity*, is pulling down toward the center of the Earth. The *skeletal* or structural system of the bridge is counteracting that force, exerting an upward force to keep it from collapsing. In your first experiment, the straws supported between the book piles were being pushed "up" by the surfaces of the books, while the cup of nails was trying to pull the straw bridge down toward Earth.

Did you notice that the straw was not absolutely rigid? Part of the downward force helped change the shape of the straw: It sagged at the middle with the weight of the cup full of nails. Just how much it bends at the middle depends partly upon how far the middle of the straw is from its supports. The farther the middle was from the book-pile supports, the greater the bend (or distortion) of the straw.

Two straws side by side should have been able to carry twice as much load.

But a beam made of *three* straws, and especially when glued together tightly, made a much stronger structure. A triangle was created in which the load carried by any one straw was more easily shared with the other two. In building construction, a beam that is made up of a number of smaller pieces fastened together is called a *laminated beam*. Laminated beams can hold more than the sum of each of their individual parts.

Surprised that one straw, cut into small pieces and placed on end, could easily carry your body weight? If you sat in a bucket hung from one soda straw stretched between two tables, it wouldn't hold you! This is because of *pressure* —the force pushing down on a surface.

You can spread a large downward force over a small area, especially if you have many small areas. If you step on one nail sticking up out of a board, it could go right through your foot. The force of your body weight is concentrated on the tiny area at the point of the nail—terrific pressure! Have you ever seen someone lying on a bed of nails? The many nails are close together so that no one nail is given enough pressure to puncture the skin. But be careful getting up and lying down!

The skeleton of a skyscraper has several vertical columns of steel. These columns carry all of the weight of the building and act just like the small pieces of straw that were glued upright. Because they carry the load vertically, there is very little distortion of the columns.

When you built the Great Bridge, you might have used a number of triangles. Triangles can share loads more easily than squares or rectangles. The triangular parts of a bridge have the same advantages in carrying a load as did your three straws fastened together. The famous American architect Buckminster Fuller pioneered the use of triangles in buildings. He called his design a *geodesic* (earth-shaped) dome. Your public library would have a picture of one. Perhaps you could try building one with straws. Imagine how it would be to live in such a house!

FOR MORE INFORMATION . . .

Places to Write and Visit

Here are some places you can write or visit for more information about mystery and magic. When you write, include your name and address and be specific about the information you would like to receive. Don't forget to enclose a stamped, self-addressed envelope for a reply.

The Discovery Center of Science and Technology
321 S. Clinton Street
Syracuse, NY 13202

The Don Harrington Discovery Center
1200 Steit Drive
Amarillo, TX 79106

Exploratorium
Palace of Arts and Sciences
3601 Lyon Street
San Francisco, CA 94123

The Magic House
516 S. Kirkwood
St. Louis, MO 63110

Further Reading about Mystery and Magic

Here are more books you can read about mystery and magic. Check your local library or bookstore to see if they have the books or can order them for you.

The Adventures of Sherlock Holmes. 4 volumes. Doyle (Avon)
Do-It-Yourself Magic. Chew (Lucky Star)
Illusions Illustrated. A Professional Magic Show for Young Performers. Baker (Lerner)
Magic by the Lake. Eager (Harcourt Brace)
Magic with Rope, Ribbon and String. Severn (McKay)
Optical Illusion Tricks and Toys. Churchill (Sterling)
Rainy Day: Magic for Wonderful Wet Weather. Forte (Incentive)
Seven-Day Magic. Eager (Harcourt Brace)

Hands-On Facts about Mystery and Magic

Did you know . . .

- mirages, such as images of cool, refreshing lakes sometimes seen by people traveling through hot deserts, are not just figments of their imaginations? Mirages are made by actual rays of light and have even been photographed.

- there was no way to store fresh meat effectively during the time of Columbus, so people often ate spoiled meat? They used spices and herbs to mask the bad taste. Yuck — please pass the hot sauce!!

- carbon dioxide (CO_2) bubbles in a liquid, such as soda water, can cause objects much heavier than the CO_2 or the liquid to rise to the top? This is because the CO_2 forms bubbles around the object that act as a kind of "lifejacket" for the object, pulling it up to the surface. Once it reaches the surface, however, the bubbles burst and the object will sink.

- electrical current can't ever really "leave home?" It must always return via an unbroken circuit to its point of origin.

- how food tastes to you depends on where it lands on your tongue? Salty and sour tastes are best tasted on the sides of your tongue, sweet things are best tasted at the tip, and the back of your tongue picks up on bitterness.

- some foods taste better when they are hot only because we can also smell them better then? Also, our taste buds are more stimulated by warm foods than by cold foods.

- royalty used to appoint "official tasters" to taste their food before they ate it? They did this because they were afraid of being poisoned by rivals.

- the noseprints of dogs are just as unique as human fingerprints? — No two are just alike!

- brine shrimp don't come from the ocean or from lakes? — They can be found in deserts. The shrimp lay their eggs in puddles created by rainfall, and then die when the water is evaporated by the sun. The eggs hatch next time there's a rainfall. Some have waited two or three years to hatch!

GLOSSARY

afterimage: an image that seems to linger in the eye after the object causing the image is no longer in view.

atom: a tiny particle of which all things are made. Every atom contains electrons, protons, and neutrons.

circuit: a complete sequence of wire or some other appropriate substance for conducting electricity.

concave mirror: a mirror whose surface is curved inward; concave mirrors are used in telescopes.

conductor: any material that allows electrons to move freely from one atom to another.

cones: photoreceptor cells in the eye that are sensitive to color.

depth perception: the eye's ability to perceive distance.

electron: negative particle of electricity that is a part of an atom.

ferromagnetic metals: metals such as iron, nickel, and cobalt that contain a high amount of magnetic iron ore.

magnetic field: the space around a magnetized object within which magnetic force can be measured.

mirage: an illusory image created by refracted light that may resemble a lake or city or some other "real" thing.

neutron: a particle of an atom that is neutral (without any electrical charge).

optic disk: a "blind spot" on your retina where the nerves and blood vessels enter it.

peripheral vision: vision to either side of the eye.

permanent magnet: a magnetic substance that maintains magnetism in one direction. The Earth is a (very large!) permanent magnet.

photoreceptors: rod and cone cells in your eye that respond to light and color.

proton: a positive particle of electricity that is a part of an atom.

retina: a lining on the inside of the eye, containing the rods and cones that are sensitive to light and color.

rods: the photoreceptor cells in the eye that are sensitive to light.

surface tension: the tension created on the surface of a liquid by molecules that tend to stay close together rather than spread apart.

taste buds: tiny specialized cells on your tongue that are linked to your brain. They react to chemicals in foods you eat, causing the brain to "taste" them.

volt: a unit to measure the force of electric current.

INDEX